SURFING

SURFING
Basic Techniques

Arnold Madison

David McKay Company, Inc.
New York

Copyright © 1979 by Arnold Madison

All rights reserved, including the right to reproduce this book, or parts thereof, in any form, except for the inclusion of brief quotations in a review.

Library of Congress Cataloging in Publication Data

Madison, Arnold.
  Surfing, basic techniques.

  SUMMARY: Introduces the fundamentals of surfing and discusses the development, types, and care of surfboards.
  1. Surfing.   [1.   Surfing]   I. Title.
GV840.S8M24   797.1'72   78-20318
ISBN 0-679-20950-6

1 2 3 4 5 6 7 8 9 10
Manufactured in the United States of America

Contents

1. *A WAVE IS A LIVING, MOVING FORCE*   *1*
2. *FROM WILIWILI TO FIBERGLASS*   *3*
3. *GETTING READY*   *11*
4. *ON THE SAND*   *23*
5. *SHOVING UNDERWAY*   *31*
6. *RIDING THE WAVES*   *39*
7. *WATCH OUT!*   *55*

1

A Wave Is A Living Moving Force

You are standing on a sliver of a board, riding a wave as high as your living room ceiling. Your lips are caked with dried salt. The sun beats on your back. Your arm and leg muscles are alert for the slightest change in the wave. And you are skimming, gliding, flying along at twenty miles an hour. You feel as free as the seagull swooping and mewing above you.

This is the moment surfers dream about and often travel hundreds of miles to experience. They practice for days, weeks, and months. They try, wipe-out, and try again. Why?

There are many reasons. First, surfing is an individual sport. There are no teammates to cover or make up for your mistakes. You either succeed or else you fail. Some people are too lazy or give up too easily to ever become surfers. But for those who work hard, success is wonderful.

Those minutes when you are alone on the board are truly your own. You are away from teachers, homework, and parents who order you to clean your bedroom. Those worries are on shore. Out on the board, it is you and the sea.

That's another reason why surfing is so popular. You are matching your skill against the greatest force on earth—the sea. You will never defeat the sea. At best, you and your rival come out even. This is why the best surfers are the people who are the most alert. Because the nature of a wave can change quickly and unexpectedly, the surfer's techniques must switch as rapidly. And by always keeping safety uppermost in your mind, you can enjoy one of the most exciting sports in the world.

2

FROM WILIWILI TO FIBERGLASS

The exact date when surfing began is not known. But historians place the sport's birth in the South Pacific Ocean. People first surfed in Polynesia—an area that includes the islands of Tahiti and Bora Bora. A number of Polynesians left these islands sometime between A.D. 800 and 1100, and headed eastward. Packed in the hulls of their giant canoes were probably boards for riding the waves. The Polynesians reached the islands of Hawaii, where they found perfect living conditions and surfing beaches. During the next 600 years, the sport and its vehicle changed and improved.

In February 1778, a British ship, commanded by Captain James Cook, sailed toward Hawaii. As the ship neared the shore, the captain and the crew gasped with shock. Ahead of them, tall men stood on the water and flew along the surface. Upon closer inspection, the newcomers spotted the large boards on which these men rode.

Early Hawaiians had two different kinds of surfing boards: the *koa* and the *olo*. Both were about twenty inches wide and five to six inches thick. They were like today's long and narrow boards, but they did not have skegs, or fins, under the tails.

The koa board, constructed of mahogany wood, was

In ancient times, Hawaiian chiefs surfed on these forty-foot waves at Makaha Beach, Oahu. Today, the International Surfing Championship meet is held here each December. (Hawaii Visitors Bureau)

used by the commoners. Today, two koa boards are on display in Honolulu's Bishop Museum. One weighs 148 pounds. The other tips the scales at 160 pounds. Clearly, the early Hawaiian surfers were strong.

The second board, or the olo, was longer than the koa. It was made from wiliwili, a wood that is almost as light as balsa. These boards were prepared during a special ceremony by the *kahunas*, or priests. The reason for such careful attention was that the olos were ridden by royalty. Special surfing beaches were set aside for the alii, or chiefs. Commoners who trespassed on these sacred sites were sentenced to death. Surfing contests among Hawaii's kings and princes were often held for large prizes. At times, the winner was given another chief's kingdom.

A printed account of Hawaiian surfing appeared for the first time in Captain James Cook's book, *A Voyage to the Pacific Ocean*. He recorded the following description:

> *As soon as they have gained . . . the smooth water beyond the surf, they lay themselves at length on their boards, and prepared for their return. . . . their first object is to place themselves on the summit of the largest surge, by which they are driven along with amazing rapidity toward the shore.*

For the next fifty-seven years, surfing was Hawaii's most popular sport. The arrival of the Boston missionaries in 1821 brought an end to surfing. Not only did the Hawaiians gamble on surfing contests, they also surfed nude. Because the religious white people believed both actions were against church teachings, they placed a ban on surfing.

For nearly a hundred years, surfing was forgotten in Hawaii except by a few people. During the early 1900s, new hotels were built along Waikiki Beach in Honolulu. Tourists were thrilled to watch the Hawaiian surfers. More surf

In the early 1900s, tourists at Waikiki Beach in Honolulu rediscovered surfing. The sport began to experience a new popularity. (Hawaii Visitors Bureau)

clubs formed, and the sport began to grow once again.

A major breakthrough in surfing came in the years before World War I. The Pacific Electric Railroad was pushing its tracks into Southern California. Ticket sales were slow. So railroad officials held surfing exhibitions at Redondo Beach, California. The surfing show then traveled all along the California coast, where thousands of eager spectators jammed the beaches.

About the same time, Hawaiian-born Duke Kahanamoku came to the United States to enter the 1912

Waterball is a sport similar to water polo, but played on surfboards. It was played in the late 1930s. (Tom Timson/ FPG)

Olympics. (He was later to hold the Olympic 100-meter swimming record from 1912 to 1924.) On his way to Chicago, Duke demonstrated surfboard riding in California. This show drew even more newcomers to the sport. Surfing had arrived in the United States to stay.

As the ranks of surfers grew, so did the complaints about the heavy pine and redwood surfing boards. They were difficult to carry, and they also caused severe injuries if they struck a person. In the 1930s, boards constructed from balsa wood were tried. But that wood was too soft and

The old surfboards, made from mahogany or redwood, were heavy as well as dangerous. (Museum of Modern Art, Film Stills Archives)

became water-logged. Although varnish was applied to the wood, this coating cracked, and the balsa took in water.

But the advantages of balsa wood made manufacturers continue to seek a way to use the light wood. Balsa boards could be carried easily by both men and women. In the water, a balsa board was very buoyant. Surfers found they could do more stunts, as well as perform faster takeoffs and turns.

Experiments were performed to see if balsa could be covered with fiberglass. This plan worked, and the new type of boards sold well. In fact, the boards were so popular

Surfing hit Hollywood in the early 1960s. Numerous motion pictures, such as "Muscle Beach Party" used surfing as story material. (Museum of Modern Art, Film Archives)

at the Malibu, California, surfing beach, the board became known as the "Malibu Board." But there were still disadvantages. When the fiberglass cracked, water seeped into the balsa, and the wood soon rotted.

During the 1950s, modern science found the answer, and the surfer's dream of a light board came true. Polyurethane foam was produced. The boards could be molded and colored by machine. Production became cheaper and faster. Sales zoomed.

The increased use of lighter materials changed the basic design of the surfing board. Balsa and foam boards now had a fixed rudder, or skeg, under the tail. This fin kept the board stable and gave the surfer greater control.

Like the seas upon which the sport is conducted, surfing now circles the entire world.

Men and women from the United States, South Africa, Australia, and many other parts of the globe are riding the waves and reaping the mental and physical rewards.

3
GETTING READY

There is no official age to start surfing. Most people, however, begin around the ages of nine and ten. Although modern surfboards are light, a certain amount of strength is needed to move them around.

Indeed, surfing is a very active sport. Your muscles, heart, and respiratory system are heavily tested while surfing. Surfboarding is not how it may seem on TV or in motion pictures. You do not calmly sit on a board, paddle out, and easily ride back to shore. Because rough waves may crash over you, you have to be able to regain normal strength after a brief rest period. As you practice, these rest periods become shorter. If a person's body cannot do this, perhaps surfing is not his or her sport. You can train your body, however, like any other athlete.

First, follow good health procedures. Get the proper amount of sleep. Keep away from junk food and eat meals which have a high protein content, such as meat and eggs. Exercise to develop your muscles. Be sure that you do the *best* exercises to prepare you for surfing. Jogging, for example, may help you get good body tone. But that is not enough for surfing. Surfers need strong shoulder, back, and arm muscles. Check with your physical education teacher in school. He or she will suggest exercises to improve the

Silly Surfer is indeed silly. He attempted to go surfing before he was in condition physically. (Dave Ross)

needed muscles. Even better, exercise in a swimming pool, a lake, or a bay.

SWIMMING

The most important skill that a surfer needs is swimming. Practice both on the surface and under water. Keep lengthening the time you can swim underwater without coming up for air. A surfer who is not an excellent swimmer is asking for trouble.

The Safety Code of the United States Surfing Association (USSA) has set standards for a beginning surfer. The USSA feels that you should be able to do the following before becoming a surfer:

* *Swim 100 yards at full strength.*
* *Swim 500 yards at a controlled pace.*
* *Remain submerged for at least 20 to 30 seconds.*
* *Have the strength to control a surfboard while paddling through at least two sets of breaking waves. (A set has from three to seven waves.)*
* *Tread water for 20 minutes, keeping your mouth above the surface. At the end of that time, swim 100 yards without stopping.*
* *Swim at least 60 feet underwater.*
* *Use a small float or kick-board. Swim at least 100 yards (using legs only) either in breast strokes (frog), scissors, or flutter.*

Can you meet those tests? If not, start practicing. No one will check to see if you have those skills. That means a surfer must have something which no one can teach him or her—common sense. For instance, common sense tells us that, like swimming, we never surf alone. Common sense also would stop you from surfing when you are not ready. To do that would be foolish and dangerous because the sea is a tremendous force. Every wave is different. From moment to moment, you must be alert for changes. Therefore, a surfer must be in the best mental and physical condition.

OTHER TYPES OF SURFING

One way to build your knowledge and your body is by surfing without a board. For example, *mat surfing* is a good way to begin. Be sure you have a strong plastic mat or raft.

Two "gremmies," or beginners, are holding kick-boards that they use to develop their kicking ability. (Black Star)

One of the best ways to begin surfing is to learn mat surfing.
(Dennis Hallinan/FPG)

Even a surf mat gets rough pounding. Mat surfing will not prepare you completely for the heavier board, but the sport is a good way to learn about waves. You will also begin to improve the techniques for steering the board while kicking. In addition, the ability to paddle while lying or kneeling on the mat will be developed. Usually, surf rafts are too flexible to stand on.

Another type of surfing is *body surfing*. People body surfed long before boards were used. This is perhaps the purest form of surfing because *you* are the surfboard.

First, select the best beach for body surfing. Swimming areas where there are quick drop-offs to deep water should be avoided. Test the beach. If you wade out a few steps and are over your head, don't body surf there. The waves break close to shore on this kind of beach. That is known as shorebreak. Because shorebreak can often be violent, find a beach where the underwater surface slopes gently downward.

Begin body surfing by standing in shallow water on the shore side, where the waves begin to break. Body surfers have to be in the right place at the right time. If you are too far inshore, a wave will break before reaching you, and the forward slope of the wave will be destroyed. If you are too far from shore, the opposite happens. The wave's face will not be steep enough to send your body sliding forward. With a little practice, you will find the best place to be.

Stand so that your back is turned to the approaching waves. Glance over your shoulder and keep a watch on what is happening. As the swell moves toward you, lean

A different kind of sea surfing is sand surfing. (Martin Inger/ FPG)

forward, with your arms outstretched, and push off with your feet. Shape yourself like the wave: head and shoulders down, legs high.

As the wave carries you ashore, keep alert. You will want to stop before the wave collapses. If you do not, you will probably end up with a mouthful of sand and a few scratches. At worst, a careless body surfer may be badly bruised or suffer a broken collar bone or displaced shoulder.

Clues will prevent injury. As you glide along, you will feel a sudden dropping. At the same time, your forward speed will increase. The time to act is now! You have about a half second before the wave crashes down. The moment you feel yourself dropping, pull out of the wave.

A pullout is simple to do. Reduce your speed so that the wave moves ahead of you. Lower one shoulder or rise up in the water. This decreases your speed. On some beaches, there is no need for a pullout. If you study the waves and see that they gently weaken, you are safe. Ride in as far as you wish.

Get solid experience in this basic form of body surfing. When you are skilled, you can try other types. You may learn how to cut right or left or even how to ride on your back or side. Fully experienced body surfers swim far out to catch incoming waves. If you do that, you have to make a decision. Should you use swimming fins? The answer is yes, if you follow two safety precautions. The fins will help you conserve energy and enjoy more body surfing each session. But be sure they fit tightly. Otherwise, the waves' actions might pull them off. Also, *never swim to a place where you would not swim without fins*. You will probably be tempted to do this. But think what would happen if you lost one or both fins. You might not have enough strength to make it back to shore.

Two girls enjoy wind surfing in the waters off Vancouver, Canada. (Black Star)

Whatever kind of body surfing you prefer, the sport will prepare you for your final goal: surfboarding.

SELECTING A SURFBOARD

Have you ever walked into a surf sporting center or flipped through *Surfer* magazine? If so, you may be confused by the many types and sizes of the board. How can you pick the right one? It would be wise not to buy a board until you have gained experience. Surfers, like other athletes, find the equipment which "feels" right for them. So, use different kinds of boards before investing money in one.

Most surfing areas have booths which rent surfboards. If you admit to the clerk that you are just beginning, the person will provide you with a beginner's board that is quite wide and has a squared end. The sides, or *rails*, are thick and round. Because a beginner's board is more stable, it will help you build confidence. As you learn the basic techniques, you can try shorter and slimmer boards. But that is in the future.

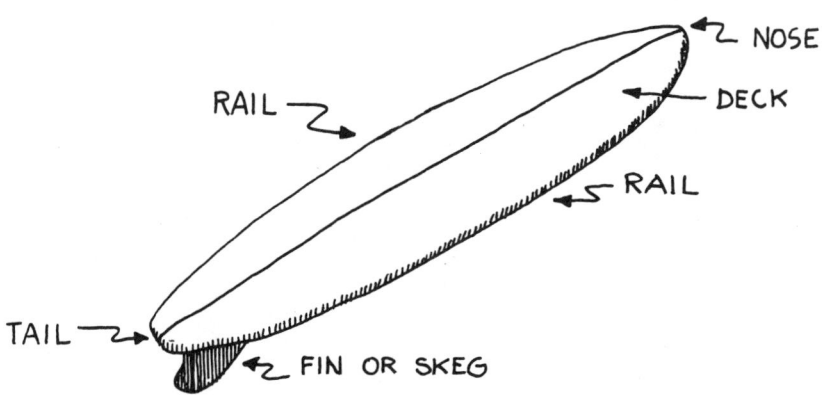

Also in the future will be the time when you buy your own board. Renting different kinds will prepare you for this. Be very careful if you decide to buy a used surfboard. If it is in good shape, the price will only be a few dollars less than a new one. Often, however, used boards have been damaged; and tiny, hairline cracks are difficult to spot.

Here are some guides you might follow when buying a board:

Surfer's Weight	Board Length	Thickness	Width
Under 100 pounds	8'9"	2¾"	21½"
100 to 120 pounds	9'0"	3"	22"
120 to 150 pounds	9'6"	3"	22"
150 to 175 pounds	9'¾"	3½"	23"

These suggestions will give you a floater-type board. This means that it is a bit oversized. But a floater is fine because the added dimensions make the board easier to paddle and catch the waves. You do not want a board that is too big, however. Although it is easily paddled, you will not be able to turn and control it in a wave. Too much width usually results in scraped arms if you attempt to paddle while on your stomach.

You now have the big three requisites for surfing: good health, excellent swimming techniques, and the proper surfboard. Let's begin learning this exciting sport.

Joyce Hoffman demonstrates how to carry a surfboard under one arm. This technique works well even with the large surfboards of the 1960s. (Ron Church/FPG)

4
ON THE SAND

Right from the first step, you will see that surfing techniques are tied in closely with safety. Surfing is a thrilling, healthy sport. But at all times, you want to consider the board, yourself, and other people. Whether you have the board on land or in the water, watch for possible danger.

CARRYING THE BOARD

Surfboards can be awkward when being carried. Should you drop the board on a hard surface, tiny cracks may ruin the board. And if the boards falls on you or another person, injury—sometimes serious—can occur. There are several techniques which will prevent accidents.

Most people prefer to carry the board under one arm. Curl your fingers under the bottom rail for greater control. Some boards are very wide, however. If your arms are too short to reach across the board, rest the board in the crook of your elbow. The top rail should lean against your shoulder. Spread the fingers of your upraised hand for better control. Another method is to carry the board on your head. First, place a folded towel between your head and the board. This will make the job more comfortable.

Some people prefer to use the buddy system while moving a board. One person carries the front end, while a second surfer holds the rear. Two boards can be transported at the same time with this method. Each surfer has a board under his or her right arm, and another under the left arm.

Silly Surfer is really in trouble because he did not wear foot gear or carry his board correctly. (Dave Ross)

Another way to safely carry a surfboard is on your head. (Ben McCall/FPG)

While carrying a board, some surfers think only about their arms and hands. Don't forget your feet. Wear sneakers or similar footwear so you do not slip in soft sand or on rocks. Never drag a surfboard through sand; dragging the front or the tail will soon wear off the board's protective coating.

Often cars bring surfboards to a beach. But some boards are too long to fit inside an automobile, so a special rack is attached to the car roof. Be certain the board is bound solidly to the carrier because the board's wide surface will catch the moving air and might cause a loosely tied board to break free. Falling to the pavement, the board would be ruined. Also, the surfboard might be crushed under the wheels of another car.

Transporting a surfboard *is* a slow process. Don't let your excitement about surfing cause you to rush. You might damage the board through carelessness.

WAXING THE BOARD

Like skis, surfboards need to be waxed. Skis, however, are waxed on the under surface, while surfboards are waxed on the upper sides. The reason for waxing is to provide better friction. Otherwise, you would continually slide off the wet, smooth surface. Apply household paraffin, the kind used in canning fruits and vegetables.

Some surfers like to wax their boards on the beach because the sun heats the wax and makes it easier to spread on the surface. First, check to see if sand is clinging to the old wax coating. If so, you may wish to carefully scrape off the old wax. The sand could irritate your feet.

You can rub or pour melted wax or "paint" the board with wax in just a few minutes. In fact, some surfers wax their boards while waiting for the next wave. *Be sure to cover the entire top surface.*

These boys have a unique way to transport their surfboards to a Los Angeles, California, beach. (Black Star)

Most surfers prefer to apply wax to their boards on the beach. The sun softens the wax and makes the application easier. (Black Star)

Many beaches have special racks where surfboards may be stored when not in use. (Robert V. Fuschetto/FPG)

If you need protection from the sun, wear a T-shirt. Never use suntan lotions on your body because they contain oil that quickly washes onto your board. Also, you may smear the oil onto the board while lying down and paddling, and cause the surfboard to become as slippery as ice.

If your wax supply is low, carry a small piece inside your swim suit. If you wax the bottoms of your feet, rather than the board, it will give you good traction on the surfboard.

You have brought your surfboard to the beach, and have waxed the top surface. Now, enter the water and experience the fun of surfing.

Silly Surfer's frantic footwork is caused by the fact that he forgot to wax his surfboard. (Dave Ross)

5

SHOVING UNDERWAY

LAUNCHING YOUR BOARD

For your protection and the surfboard's safety, you want to select the best launching site. Check the shoreline carefully. If you have a smooth, sandy beach, you should have no problems. However, are there sea animals, such as crabs, urchins, or mussels that might bruise your feet? Are the waves breaking close to shore? Be sure your board does not get carried away by them. Do you have to walk over rocks to reach the launching spot? Stepping over and on stones might cause you to lose your balance and drop the board. Also, keep the board's skeg turned up while walking over the rocks. You will then avoid snagging the fin on a stone. Proceed through the launching process with care.

If the breaking surf is light, walk out, holding the board's nose high so that a wave will not catch it and drag it from your arms. Also, point the board straight ahead. If the board is turned, a wave might strike broadside, causing the board to broach, or turn sideways and over. This action would yank the board free. And you would probably be struck by your own board.

When you have reached water deep enough to float the board, set it on the water. If there are underwater rocks, keep the board upside down until you are beyond them. This will protect the fin.

There are two means of keeping the board under control while you are launching. First, grip both rails near the nose, and remember to raise the nose above incoming waves. The second method is to hold the left side about the middle of the board, with your right hand grasping the tail. By doing this, your right hand will push down the tail so that incoming waves will pass under the nose.

When you wade into the water, never shove the board ahead of you so that it floats untended. Keep the board under control at all times until you reach a spot where the surf is calm or appears glassy. This is the best place to mount the board.

MOUNTING THE BOARD

The safest way to mount the board is from the side. Point the nose toward shore so the tail is aimed at the approaching waves. Grip each side near the board's middle. Then, in three stages, climb on: (1) Lower your midsection onto the board; (2) Swing one leg on; (3) Place your second leg so that you are fully on the board.

You are now lying prone along the center of the board. Your toes should be about ten inches from the tail. The lower part of your ribs are approximately mid-board. To check if you are correctly placed, study the board's nose. If the front tip is about two inches out of the water, you are set perfectly. If the board is too high, inch forward. Should the nose be in the water, slide backwards until the nose rises. If the board is tilted sideways, move in the opposite direction. You were not exactly centered on the surfboard.

This process is called *trimming* the board. When you are positioned correctly, and the board's nose is two inches above the water, the board is in trim.

PADDLING

There are two positions for paddling—prone and kneeling. Beginners should practice paddling in the prone position first. All your attention can then be given to the board. When you gain experience, try paddling in a kneeling position. This is a bit more difficult because you have to worry about your body as well as the board.

When you first learn *prone paddling*, remain in calm water. Keep your legs together and elbows bent. Raise your chest so that your weight is on your stomach, lower ribs, and thighs. Bend your elbows and cup each hand. Cupping your hands will give you greater resistance as you paddle. Be sure to use both hands at the same time.

Paddling is like throwing a baseball overhand. You reach up and forward, then dig your cupped hands into the water. Take a deep stroke and pull your hands back. The procedure is similar to canoe paddling. You should *feather* your hands. This means turning your hands sideways at the end of a stroke so that they can glide easily through the water. Feathering also helps you to bring your arms out of the water with less effort.

When you first practice paddling, you will tire easily. You might take a break by practicing to mount your board. Then, when you feel rested, return to paddling. The more you work out, the more developed your muscles will become. You will find that your paddling sessions last longer without tiring you as quickly.

Once your endurance and paddling techniques have improved, try *knee paddling*. This will mean giving more attention to maintaining balance. Again, remain in calm water when first attempting this type of paddling. You may even find knee paddling more comfortable than prone paddling because there is no pressure on your ribs and stomach.

Knee paddling is actually a rocking-forward-and-back motion. You first sit back on your heels. As you begin to reach out to begin the paddle, your body bends forward. You dig into the water and rock back. By doing this, you are using both you arm muscles and body movement to add power to the paddle.

Special techniques are needed when paddling down a wave. You may have to move the center of balance forward or backward by shifting your body in those directions. Moving the balance point forward increases the downward tilt of the board, which will slide faster down the wave. Moving your weight back lessens the slide angle and helps preventing *pearling*. Pearling occurs when the board's nose digs into the water. The board then slows and even stops, and the surfer falls into the water.

There are other methods of paddling. You can sit with your feet on the board, for example, but you won't get speed. Still, this technique can be helpful while staying in position for an approaching wave. Or you can straddle the board with your feet in the water. Moving the legs in a circular pattern will propel the board, but you will not gain much speed or distance.

TURNING THE BOARD

Once you have developed the skill to propel the surfboard, you need to learn turning techniques for greater control.

For slight turns, a stronger stroke with only one arm will make the board angle in the opposite direction. Or you can drag one arm or leg in the water. If you drag your right leg, the board turns right. To turn left, drag your left arm or leg. Leaning in the direction you wish to go will also cause a slight turn.

Perhaps the most important turn to master is a rapid 180° turn. Many surfers face out to sea while waiting for the best wave. As it approaches, they swing their boards around quickly. To do this, sit on the tail end of the board. Two-thirds of the board should be out of the water. The tail then becomes the pivot point around which the board will turn. To swing left, your legs should rotate clockwise through the water. A right turn is obtained by rotating your legs counterclockwise. You will be surprised at how swiftly the board turns once you have mastered this technique.

PADDLING OUT

Even experienced surfers spend much time studying the waves before paddling out. The sea changes from day to day and even from hour to hour.

At times, the waves come ashore in a pattern. By detecting that pattern, you will be able to figure out the best time to paddle out. For example, you may see that the waves come in sets followed by a calm period. Why fight the heavy waves? In a few minutes, the water will be more easily conquered. At other times, the waves roll in with no lull between the sets. Try to find a channel of smoother water to paddle through, or else paddle around the end of the break.

Inexperienced surfers are urged not to attempt crashing through big, rough breakers. So know your own skill at all times. Choose the days when the waves are small and weak, and use prone paddling. Paddle directly into the oncoming waves. When you reach an unbroken wave, paddle over it.

If the wave has broken, paddle into the white, foamy

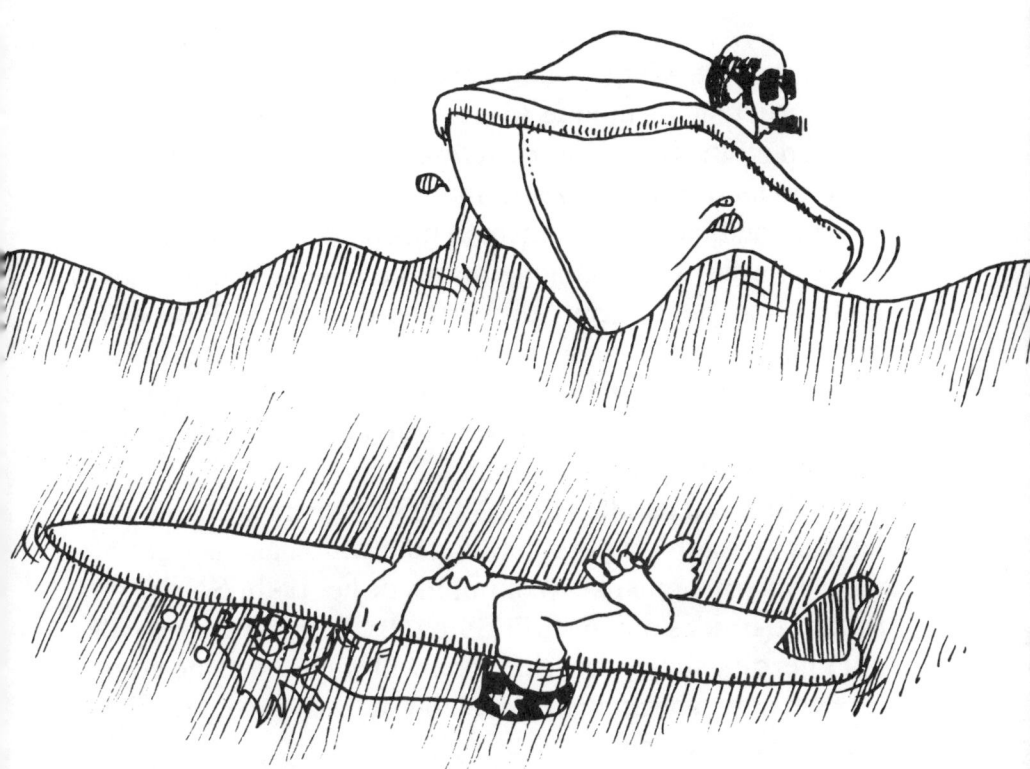

Silly Surfer is doing the turn-turtle technique perfectly, but at the worst possible time. Always keep approaching boats in view. (Dave Ross)

water. But, as your board makes contact, push up with your arms as if doing a pushup in a gym. This lifts your body off the board and offers less resistance for the water. The white water flows underneath you and off the board, but your board will not lose much speed. Also, you will avoid getting your face washed by that white water. Your board will then slide into the trough behind the wave. Lower yourself to the board and continue paddling.

As this surfer met an oncoming wave, he did a push-up to lessen resistance. (Richard Stelhorn/FPG)

If you see a large, dangerous wave approaching, there is a particular technique to use. Rather than risk getting washed off the board, you can *turn turtle*. Keep the board's nose pointed into the wave, and wrap your arms and legs around the board. Lock them in place. Take a deep breath and roll over, while hanging onto the board. You are now underwater, holding onto the surfboard which is above you. Your body will act as a sea anchor and prevent the board from being washed back to shore. Also, this action is protection for you. If there are stray boards in that wave, you will not be struck by them.

When you paddle out to actual surf, there is an unwritten rule to follow: a person riding the wave has the right of way; everyone must keep out of his or her path. So paddle toward the sides of the surfing area. By doing that, you will not interrupt someone's ride. You will want the same courtesy when you begin your ride. Now, let's shove out for that important first ride.

6
RIDING THE WAVES

The basic techniques you have practiced are important for the real fun—riding the waves! Again, there are steps to follow. A person does not begin by paddling out and standing for a quick, easy ride to shore. If you try that, you will find yourself in the water, swimming to catch your board.

RIDING PRONE

You may be tempted to head out immediately to where other surfers are lined up. To *learn* riding, however, stay in the area where the waves are broken. The waves should be running from about two to three feet high.

Paddle out there, and have your board parallel to shore. This will give you a good chance to watch the waves from all directions. When a swell comes toward you, turn the board's nose directly toward the shore. Begin paddling as if trying to get away from that wave. Your board should be moving at a good speed as the broken wave catches up to you. The timing will have to be practiced. If you find yourself reaching shore ahead of the wave, you began paddling too soon.

When you suddenly feel the wave take hold of the surfboard, stop paddling and let the wave do all the work. That's what all this practice has been for. If you have caught that broken wave well, you can ride all the way into shore. But that is not wise. You want to avoid having the board's skeg drag through sand or rocks. End your ride before there is any possible danger.

After several prone rides, you may be anxious to advance to kneeling rides. Even if prone riding seems mild, continue until you have completed fifteen to twenty such rides. There are many skills to be perfected during these sessions. First, you will improve your timing. Also, as you will see, waves are not always the same. Changing wave conditions will mean varying your techniques. You will learn to trim your board at times during these rides.

Keep practicing your prone riding until you have truly mastered the technique. Then move onto the next step.

KNEELING DURING THE RIDE

To advance to a kneeling ride, stay in the section where the waves are broken. The trick is getting from a prone position to one where you are kneeling. Remain flat until the broken wave has caught the board. As the wave carries you forward, continue to grip the board's railings. Pull first one knee forward and then the second. Now you are kneeling and still holding the sides. Do a few rides in this fashion until you feel confident.

Then try removing your hands from the rails. Stretch your arms out to the sides and balance your board like a high-wire acrobat. If the board becomes unbalanced, quickly grab the sides again. When you have re-trimmed the board, release your hold on the rails. You will have to try many such rides before doing them well.

You can also practice turning without holding onto the board. Shift your weight slightly in the direction you wish to turn. That side of the board will sink lower, and the nose will angle in that direction.

Soon, you will be riding your board in a no-hands, kneeling position with great success.

STANDING

Before you stand on a surfboard, you must decide if you are going to surf with your right or left foot forward. There's a simple test you can make. Find a smooth surface, then run and slide a few feet. The foot that is in front as you come to a halt is probably the one that will work best for you. Most surfers prefer their left foot forward, while others can surf with either foot in the front position.

Begin the standing practice on the beach. Place your board on the sand, making sure the skeg is dug deeply into the sand. If the fin is resting on the surface, you may harm it when standing on the board.

Now, lay flat on the board. Move into a kneeling position, and then stand up. Practice this a few times. Then see if you can speed up the process by coming to a crouch and moving right up on your feet. Use your arms to keep balanced. When you feel satisfied that you can stand on the beached board, find an area of calm water.

Return to the first steps you followed on the beach. Remember that the conditions are going to be different. That nice, steady beached board will wobble now. Begin in the prone position, then come up to a kneeling or crouch, and finally rise straight up on your feet. If the board seems on the verge of tipping, drop down to a kneeling position. Get the board under control once again, then continue practicing.

For the basic stand-up position, your feet should be about eighteen inches apart, with your back foot almost at a right angle to the board's center line. Your body can face directly forward or at a 45° angle to the center line. Your arms should be outstretched and moving to keep balance.

This is a *suggested* stance. As you do more surfing, you may change this position slightly to one which suits you better.

Trimming the board while riding is done by shifting your body weight. If the board nose appears too high, shift your weight to the front foot. Should the board be too low, move the weight to the back foot. A more popular means of trimming the board is using your "riding" or front foot. Moving the riding foot forward lowers a high board and increases speed. Sliding the same foot back will raise the nose and slow the board. At other times, both feet advance or edge backward. Maintain your normal stance while doing this. When riding a wave, these actions with your feet are done quickly and constantly.

THE FIRST RIDE

At this point you have developed your swimming skills and mastered the basic techniques on broken waves. Now let's join the surfers who are riding unbroken waves.

Paddle out to the *line-up*, where other surfers are waiting for good waves. Remember the courtesy rule: the surfer riding a board always has the right of way. So paddle to the line-up from the side. Study the positions of the other surfers to see how much space to leave between you and them.

When you first ride the unbroken waves, return to the beginning techniques. Your first rides will be prone. When you have captured that skill, try kneeling rides. Finally, advance to standing. But don't be in a hurry to get on your

A young surfer at Nauset Beach, Cape Cod, practices getting to his feet on the surfboard. (Black Star)

feet because there is much to be learned from prone and kneeling rides on unbroken waves.

For your first ride, have your board pointed at the oncoming waves. Wait for a large one. Then spin your board around, using the tail as the pivot point. Lie prone, and watch the wave over your shoulder. As it approaches, dig in and begin paddling. The wave is still behind you, and your board is at a right angle to the incoming swell. When that

One method of steering is by dragging a hand on the side of the surfboard. (Black Star)

swell comes, the board's nose dips and the tail rises. Your ride has begun.

Now that you have caught the wave, turn and lean away from the breaking portion. The feeling you have could be compared to flying, although most surfers claim there is nothing like it.

Don't be disappointed if you do not make it all the way to shore on the first try. You may need to learn to recover from a possible wipe-out. To do this, turn back into the wave and shift your weight to the back of the board.

You've now experienced that first ride. Soon, you will be kneeling and, finally, standing. At that point, there will be finer techniques to learn and to practice.

STEERING

You have already learned the basic methods of steering: (1) leaning; (2) changing stroke power; (3) dragging an arm or leg in the water. Steering while standing is more difficult because there are only four contact areas between you and the board, the heel and ball of each foot.

Many types of turns are used by surfers. But basically, they all depend on two techniques of shifting your feet. The *leaning* or *tilt turn* is an easy swing to the right or left. You do not move your feet. All you do is shift your weight. Bicycle riders use this technique all the time. They turn the wheel of the bike and lean in the direction of the turn. The same method applies to surfing.

For example, if you wish to turn the board right, lean forward so that most of your weight rests on the balls of your feet. Now twist your body to the right. The weight of your body will be off-center and to the right, causing the right rail of the surfboard to sink a bit deeper. The board will slowly swing right.

If you need to turn left, lean backward toward the left

Silly Surfer has learned too late that a surfer must leave a wave before the wave collapses. (Dave Ross)

side; and place all your weight on your heels. Now, rotate, or twist, your body to the left without moving your feet. The left rail will sink down, and the board will turn to the left.

Often, however, you will need to make sharper turns. At those times, employ the *rear foot*, or *tail-down turn*. The success of this turn depends on your "turning" your rear foot. Rather than shifting your weight, move that foot closer to the right or left rail.

For instance, if you wish to make a sharp left turn, move your rear foot to the left rear side of the board. Put all

Wipeout! (Black Star)

Stall a surfboard by raising the nose high from the water's surface. (Black Star)

your weight on that foot as you twist your body to the left. The surfboard will angle sharply left. To do a quick right turn, reverse the procedure. Shift your weight to your turning foot, which is on the right rear side of the surfboard. Rotate your body to the right. Immediately, the board will swerve right.

Once a turn—slow or abrupt—has been completed, fast movement is needed. Get your board trimmed quickly, otherwise you will turn too far and possibly have a spill.

FALLING AND ENDING YOUR RIDE

Even the best surfers have wipe-outs or fall from their boards. In the beginning, you may feel foolish when this happens. Don't. There are times when you *want* to fall. If a wave is too steep or collapses, it is safer to end your ride.

If there is time, you may wish to *stall* the board. This is a term which comes from flying. When a plane angles up too sharply without enough speed, the aircraft stalls. The engine keeps running, but the lift under the wings is lost, and the plane starts falling. The same goes for surfing. You can stall a surfboard by getting the nose high in the air.

Stalling can be done by shuffling back toward the rear of the board. But don't shuffle too far! You may shuffle off the rear end. Or you can drop to a kneeling or sitting position far back on the board. This action, too, will raise the board's nose. Some surfers stall a board by crouching on the rear. As the board's front end rises, the surfer falls forward. Gripping the railings, he or she is now in position for a prone ride.

A stall is also used to end your ride near the shore. You do not want to be caught in a crashing wave. So, as your ride is about to end, make a sharp rear right or left turn. The wave will move ahead, as you stall the board to a halt.

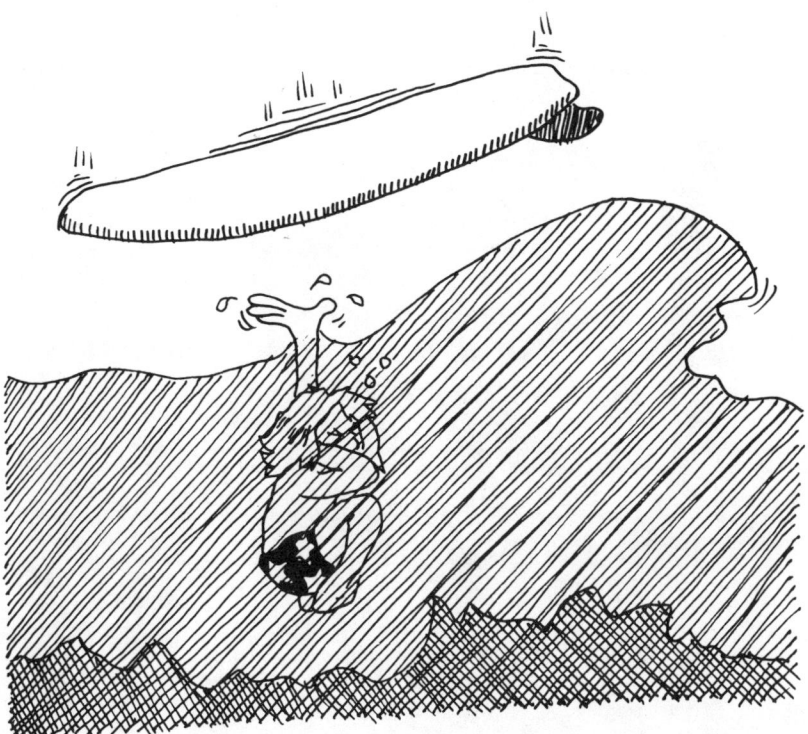

Silly Surfer has assumed the best possible position while underwater. But he should not have his hand above the surface. The board will crash down upon his arm. (Dave Ross)

Still another way to escape danger is to jump backwards off either side. Keep an arm outstretched so you can grab the board before it gets free.

When you have to leave the board fast, walk or run to the rear and dive. If you do this or accidentally fall, try to stay underwater as long as possible. Your surfboard is now being churned about by the waves. Lightweight boards can be tossed forward or backward great distances. Therefore, you can never be certain where the loose board may be.

Remain underwater, but pull your knees up to your chest because there may be underwater rocks or coral.

Leave hotdogging to the expert surfers. (Museum of Modern Art, Film Archives)

Bend your head forward until your chin touches your chest. Spread your hands over the base of your skull, and bring the elbows to the sides of your face. Doing this will protect the most open parts of your body. You are not completely safe, however. As you begin to rise to the surface, push an arm up like a periscope. The hand is "seeing" if a surfboard is directly above you.

This chapter has dealt with the important skills of

surfing. As you practice and perfect these techniques, you will be able to handle more difficult ones.

For now, leave *hot-dogging*, or performing tricks, for the very experienced surfers. Some people like to *hang-five* or *hang-ten*. Doing that means standing on the very front of the board so either five or all ten toes hang over the nose. These stunts require perfect timing and much skill.

Meanwhile, enjoy surfing and polish up those basic techniques. Your rides will be fun and safe.

A surfer in North Carolina. (Black Star)

7

WATCH OUT!

There are two qualities every surfer needs. One is close attention to safety at all times, and the other is the ability to plan ahead. Combining the two will prevent needless accidents and insure great times with your surfboard.

Newspapers sometimes carry stories about a surfer's injuries: A young man is attacked by a shark in California; a young woman collides with another surfer in Long Island, New York. Often, such injuries might have been prevented. In fact, the majority of reported surfing accidents could have been avoided. At times, the Coast Guard issues warnings when sharks have been spotted off shore. Or beach officials may post notices that the surf is too rough. For a beginner or even an experienced surfer to ignore such warnings is foolish and an invitation to trouble.

Other accidents occur because a surfer was not alert to nearby surfers or bathers or attempted to surf on a wave which was too large to handle. And sometimes an individual ignores the signs of a pending wipe-out.

NATURAL DANGERS

Possibly the most widespread danger is that of *sharks*. They are especially dangerous in waters off Australia. But sharks are also found along the east and west coasts of the United States and in the Gulf of Mexico. If you cut yourself while surfing, get out of the water. Sharks have a keen sense of smell and can detect blood at great distances. Blood attracts sharks. Also, do not bring food out on your surfboard.

If you spot the familiar dorsal fin, head for shore as quickly and calmly as possible. Do this even if you hear someone call, "Shark!" Find out later if they were playing a joke. And, of course, *never* try to be funny and shout a phony warning.

Watch out for *rip currents*. These occur when too much water piles up in the shallow areas along shore. Water seeks its natural level. Therefore, this extra water flows out to sea, and forms strong currents. A rip current is usually twenty yards wide and moves about five miles per hour. This current can be spotted by the color of the water.

Silly Surfer did not heed the Coast Guard's warnings that sharks had been sighted off shore. Now what is he going to do? (Dave Ross)

Because the rip current picks up sand as it moves out from shore, the water is lighter in color than the surrounding areas. Standing on shore, you will see a triangle of lighter water or foam pointing out to sea.

Should you become caught in a rip current, do not try to fight your way out. Drift along in the current until it weakens farther out to sea. You will not be dragged a tremendous distance out. Then swim ashore. The real danger occurs when swimmers tire themselves out by struggling, and become too tired to reach shore. Although some surfers purposely ride their boards out, powered by a rip current, this is not a wise idea.

Cold water and fatigue can happen if water temperatures drop and the wind blows. Wet surfers, sitting on their boards, are affected quickly. They begin shivering, their hands and feet feel numb, and their muscles become stiff. These reactions weaken their ability to surf safely.

Don't try to prove you are tough. Get out of the water or wear a wet suit. Unless the water temperature is in the fifties or lower, you need only wear the top half of the wet suit. For very cold water, use the top and bottom for full protection. The comfort and safety are worth the price of a wet suit.

RULES OF CONDUCT

Surfing areas along our beaches can become crowded. Therefore, surfers have agreed upon a set of rules to protect themselves and other people at the beach.

* **As you paddle out, avoid the paths of incoming surfers.** *This has been mentioned before. But the rule is an important one. Courtesy and safety will result when you follow this suggestion.*

* **Surf at your own level of skill.** Many surfing accidents can be traced to thoughtlessness, such as a surfer attempting to ride a wave or to use a technique that he or she could not handle.

* **Avoid other swimmers or bathers.** Most beaches have a special surfing area. Stay well within that space, but keep an eye open. Some swimmers—especially young children—may have mistakenly entered the surfing section.

* **Keep your board in good shape.** Constantly inspect your board to see if there are rough or jagged sections which might cut you or others. Also, keep the board well waxed at all times.

* **Don't take off in front of an approaching rider.** Not only is this rude, but it is dangerous. The person coming toward you might not be able to turn fast enough. A collision is possible.

* **Don't force another surfer to drop out of a wave.** Waves, too, can be crowded. If so, the person in front and the farthest ahead of the break should avoid cutting back. If the individual does cut back, he or she could collide with the other surfers.

* **Be aware at all times.** The rule has been stressed throughout this book. But awareness will mean safety. Watch the wave conditions. Know where the other surfers are at all times. Check your path ahead. Expect the unexpected.

These basic rules are easy to follow. Doing so will not rob you of any fun or enjoyment. All the excitement of this sport will be yours as it was for the chiefs of old Hawaii. You may not bet a kingdom on the outcome of a ride, but you will be reaping the rewards of this thrilling, outdoor sport.